Chrismons

**AN EXPLANATION OF THE SYMBOLS
ON THE CHRISMON TREE AT**

**THE ASCENSION LUTHERAN
CHURCH IN DANVILLE, VIRGINIA**

An Original   Trade Mark

by

Frances Kipps Spencer

Chrismons™

Scripture quotations, unless otherwise noted in the text, are from the Revised Standard Version of the Bible, copyright 1946 and 1952 by the Division of Christian Education of the National Council of Churches.

Ninth Printing

Published by

Ascension Lutheran Church

314 West Main Street

Danville, VA 24541

ISBN 978-0-9715472-4-7

Website www.chrismon.org

chrismonsministry@gmail.com

The Chrismon Tree originated in this church in 1957. From that beginning, the idea has spread to Christians all over the world. Our congregation continues to help any who wish to use this means of praising and proclaiming the Christ.

The evergreen tree, which symbolizes the eternal life which our Savior has won for us, is a background for tiny white lights and white and gold Chrismons. The lights speak of Him Who is the Light of the world, and the Chrismons (CHRISt + MONogram) proclaim the Name, the Life, and the saving Acts of Jesus the Christ.

Some Chrismons are simple copies of symbols of Christianity from its earliest days; others are new explanations of God's never-changing presence in our ever-changing world; and some are combinations of several elements, old and new. We hope that these pages will help you understand the truths that the tree proclaims.

MAY THESE SUMBOLS CONTINUALLY REMIND YOU OF GOD'S
GREATEST GIFT TO US ALL, JESUS CHRIST.

Welcome to Ascension Lutheran Church

The Public is Cordially invited to view the Chrismons Tree during the Advent and Christmas season.

We most certainly would like for you and your loved ones to worship with us during these seasons and throughout the church year.

We would like to thank all those who through the years have given their time and talent to make this publication possible including the following:

PHOTOGRAPHS by Mrs. Janice Jones unless otherwise identified

PUBLICATION: Gail K. Bengston
Gary L. Bengston
Ronald I. Fisher
Undine H. Kipps
Martha Gray J. McCauley
Robert V. Shaver
Harry W. Spencer
Margaret S. Witherspoon

Front cover: 2004 Chrismons Tree
Photography © Alan Dalton

CONTENTS

THE CRECHE

On the lowest branches of our tree, our youngest visitors will find the Crèche. Although most Chrismons are symbolic, this one is pictorial. Surrounding the manger scene are miniature size Chrismons.

Another Chrismon, this time a symbolic rendering of the crèche, is illustrated on this page. A Chi becomes a manger topped with a crown to suggest the King Who lay in it. The shape of the Rho reminds us of the crook that was carried by the Child's first visitors. (See page 10.) This entire design also proclaims the Child's mission: The Christ was to be the Good *Shepherd for all mankind.*

ELEMENTS OF THE CHRISMONS

Chrismons proclaim our Lord Jesus Christ through the use of symbols. Some of these visible signs for the invisible antedate the Lord's historical life. Others were used by the Christ Himself and His contemporaries to describe His nature and mission . Over the years, still other symbols for the Savior have been developed by His followers. This process has continued up to, and we hope through, the present . Teachers and artists and preachers attempt to lead, through the symbol, to a consideration of deeper ideas and truths.

These symbols, which are interdenominational and the heritage of all Christians, are the elements of the Chris-mons. Although a few ornaments on our tree utilize only one or two elements to present their message, most Chrismons combine several signs, symbols, pictures, and/or types. Designs differ in the way that they unite the various elements so that each Chrismon presents its unique message . But the basic signs and symbols remain the same. This section describes the individual parts that make up a Chrismon 's meaning.

Two elements unite to form the above design: A Chi (X), the first letter of Christ in Greek, is superimposed on a cross. Christ and the Cross-can we separate them?

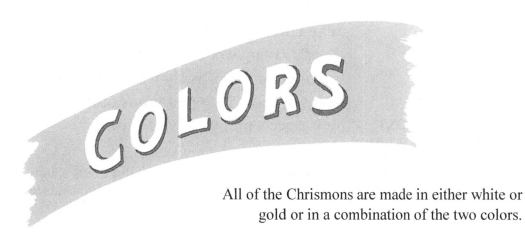

All of the Chrismons are made in either white or gold or in a combination of the two colors.

WHITE, the Liturgical color for Christmas, suggests the innocence, purity , and perfection of our Savior. In our culture, it is the color of joy. Scripture often uses white to portray purity and equates it with light to denote completeness. *Isaiah 1:18; Mark 9:3, Revelation 20 :11.*

GOLD, as a symbol for the glory and majesty of God and the Son of God, is also derived from Biblical usage. *Exodus 25:11 ff; Revelation 1:13-16; 21:18-21.*

For emphasis, certain Chrismons show a touch of **RED** to remind us of the blood of Christ by which we are saved. *Hebrews 9:14.*

Symbols marked with this spot of red are the pelican-in- her-piety, the sacrificial lamb, and some crosses.

Although few people who see our tree are aware of it, we add other colors to Chrismons when their use is necessary to the meaning of a symbol :

The stone, which represents the tribe of Judah, in the Jesse tree must be **GREEN**. *Exodus 1:1, 2 ; 28:18.*

The burnt out wicks on the lamps of the five foolish virgins are **BLACK** to differentiate them from the still burning lamps of the wise virgins. *Matthew 25:1 ff.*

LATIN CROSS
Most widely used form today.

The CROSS is, of course, always a reminder of our Lord's saving work of redeeming mankind through His sacrifice for our sins, by which we receive forgiveness and salvation. Different forms of the cross point to various aspects of our Savior's work.

GREEK CROSS: While the leg of the Latin Cross is longer than the arms, all parts of the Greek cross are equal. The balanced form, more adapt- able in design, was widely used by early Greeks.

CRUX GAMMADIA: When the edges of the Greek Cross are emphasized, four Greek Gammas appear.

CROSS TRIUMPHANT (OF VICTORY): Triumph of the Gospel through the world; Christ glorified.

CROSS WITH ORB: Artists of ten show our Lord holding a cross-topped orb: The earth and heaven in the Lord's hands; the world united in Christ .

TAU CROSS: The "T" shape suggests Moses' staff and evokes the Messianic promises.

SERPENT ON TAU CROSS: The bronze serpent on the staff by which the Lord saved Israel: A type of the crucifixion. Numbers 21:9; John 3:14.

CROSS IN ETERNITY

CELTIC CROSS: The circle may represent the sun or eternity, as in the cross above. But some think that the circle was merely a support for the heavy stone arms of the original crosses.

EASTERN CROSS (RUSSIAN): We offer one of several interpretations: The top bar-the superscription; the bottom bar-the footrest.

JERUSALEM CROSS: Cross of Crusader kings; Five crosses-five wounds of our Lord. Or, prophecies (Taus) climaxed in Jesus' crucifixion near Jerusalem (large cross). Since then, Christians have carried the Gospel to the four corners of the word (corner crosses).

The center cross alone, **CROSS POTENT**: The Savior's spiritual and physical healing powers.

Adjectives added to a cross may describe the decorative termination of its members. Arms of the **CROSS CROWNED** end in crowns to suggest Christ's crown of glory. *NIKA* - Greek for Victor. *Hebrews 2:9.*

Paired **LATIN CROSSES FUSILÉE**, one entwined with an Alpha, another with an Omega. (Fusilée-spindle; diamond-shaped.) *Revelation 1:8.*

CROSS FUSILÉE COUPED with a monogram of the name Jesus. (Couped-cut.) The circle around the Greek monogram for Christ makes this cross Fusilée Couped resemble the ANSATE or Looped Cross.

CROSS PATTÉE w/SCROLLS: Salvation proclaimed in the four Gospels: Winged man-Matthew; Winged Lion-Mark; Winged Ox-Luke; Eagle-John .

Nature and artifacts reveal hidden crosses. **SOUTHERN CROSS**: A constellation of four stars seen in the Southern hemisphere. **EYE OF GOD** *(Ojo de Dios):* A pre-Columbian art form reveals a cross in its weave.

From the HEAVENS

THE UNIVERSE: One triangle suggests the One God Whom we know by the acts of the three Persons. Another triangle reminds us that no man has seen this same God. When the triangles come into conjunction, we see the CREATOR 'S STAR and God's visible creation. Note a ROSE on one of the planets circling one of the suns-earth in the configuration that presaged our Savior's birth. Since the day that Christ Jesus was physically with us, our knowledge of the world has expanded to include the universe. Yet we still point to the events in His Life as our justification.   *Exodus 33:20; Psalm 8; Hebrews 2.*

SUN OF RIGHTEOUSNESS:

About twenty four hundred years ago, the prophet Malachi compared the Messiah to the sun, the brightest thing in his or our world. A representation of the sun which is centered with our Lord's monogram recalls the prophecy, "But for you who fear my name the sun of righteousness shall rise, with healing in its wings." *Malachi 4:2.*

STARS, formed by crosses set at various angles, show the close relationship between the birth and death of our Redeemer.
The number of points that a star has may indicate a specific meaning:

FOUR POINTS: CROSS ETOILE (Star Cross).

FIVE POINTS: EPIPHANY STAR; Our Savior; Manifestation of the Son.
Matthew 2:1-11.

SIX POINTS: CREATOR'S STAR; The Father; Six days of creation.
Exodus 20:11.

SEVEN POINTS: GIFTS OF THE SPIRIT; Holy Spirit.
Revelation 5:12.

EIGHT POINTS: HOLY BAPTISM: Regeneration.
I Peter 3:20, 21.

Several MULTI-POINTED STARS: Heaven.

and the EARTH

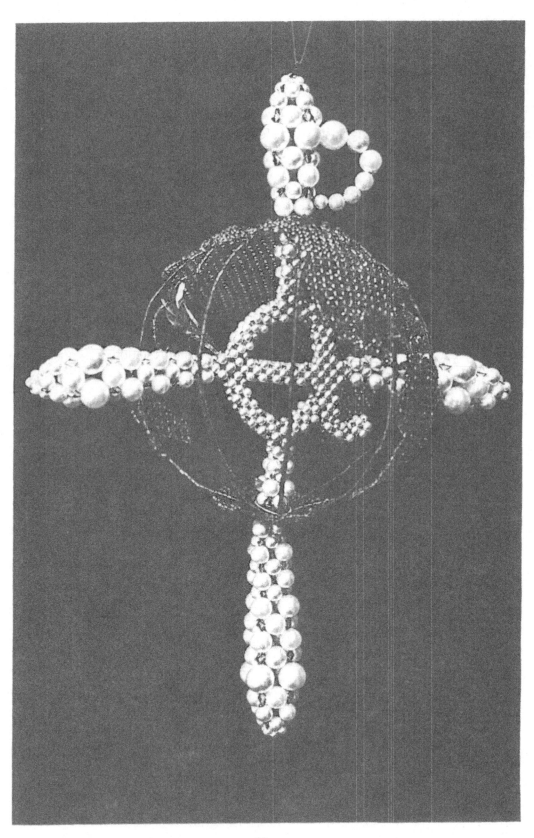

WATER: "If anyone thirst, let him come to me and drink." John 7:37. Biblical writers and Jesus Himself often used water to symbolize His life-giving nature. *Isaiah 55:1; John 4:10 ff; Revelation 21:6; 22:17.*

At times, water may refer to Baptism or, by extension, the Holy Spirit. *Acts 8:36 .*

FLAMES: The Holy Spirit on the day of Pentecost. *Acts 2:1-4.*

ROCK: Scriptural applications of this figure for the Christ must be interpreted in context. Stumbling stone-*Romans 9:33*; Source of living water-*I Corinthians 10:4*; A good foundation-*Luke 6:48.*

Scripture frequently employs parts of the body to describe "God the Father Almighty, Maker of heaven and earth ," We use these same figures on our tree.

References to the **HAND** suggest the creative act, supportive care, judgment, and power. *Exodus 15:6; Deuteronomy 11:2; Ezra 8:22; Psalms 16:11; 18:35; 104:28; 139:10; Habakkuk 3:4; Luke 1:66; Acts 7:50.*

The "**EYE OF GOD**" connotes loving care and watchful judgment. *Judges 18:6; Psalms 17:8; 33:18; Ezekiel 20:17 .*

THE INCARNATION (At the left):   CHRIST IN THE WORLD, THROUGH IT, AND BEYOND IT. At the crucial point of the cross, inside the globe of the world, two Greek letters are superimposed: Theta (Θ), the first letter in the Greek word for God, and Alpha (a), the first letter in the word for man.

PLANTS & FLOWERS

PROPHECY
Some people consider Isaiah 's prophecy, "The desert shall . . . blossom . . ." (35:1) a Messianic Promise. Thus, the flower became a symbol of the Messiah. But since different translations call the flower a rose, lily, crocus, or jonquil, all became figures for Christ. Years of usage established certain meanings. **MESSIANIC ROSE** (stylized, five-petaled): Messianic Promise. **ROSE** (natural): Our Lord's virgin mother Mary, His human birth, or His Humanity. **LILY**: The Virgin Mary. **CROCUS & JONQUIL**:
From recent translations and therefore not yet widely known.

LIFE AND TEACHINGS
Because certain plants played a Lord's Life, these plants became symbols for the events.

PALM: Christ's triumphant ride into Jerusalem. John 12:13.

WHEAT & GRAPES: Bread and wine, Body and Blood of our Lord. Luke 22:14 ff.

THORNS: Our Savior's crown of suffering. Mark 15:17.

Since Jesus taught in terms familiar to His listeners, He drew some illustrations from plants of the Holy Land .

ANEMONES: Probably the "lilies of the field" cited to describe the Father's loving care of His children. Matthew 6:28.

WHEAT & WEEDS: "Sons of the kingdom... sons of the evil one." Matthew 13:24 ff.

WHEAT: "Bread of life." John 6:35

VINE: "I am the vine, you are the branches." John 15.

WITNESS BY THE BRANCHES

Since Biblical times, our Lord's disciples associated other flowers with His person. Generally, the linkage occurs because of a blossom's specific nature.

DAISY: A flower of simplicity - the innocence of the Christ Child.

DOGWOOD: Bracts set to form a cross with reddish-brown markings remind us of the Crucifixion.

GLADIOLUS: The Incarnation. The sword plant. John 1:14; Hebrews 4:12.

LILLY: The Resurrection. Probably based on the emergence of the flower from the seemingly dead bulb.

LILY - OF - THE - VALLEY: Its low growth suggests Christ's humility.

LOTUS: From roots in the mud, the stem rises through the waters to support a flower of beauty and purity.

PASSION FLOWER: Its markings recall events of our Lord's Passion.

SHAMROCK: Three leaflets on one stem illustrate the Triune God.

CREATURES Of The Earth

The **FISH**, an ancient symbol for the Christ, was a secret sign during early Christianity's persecutions. On catacomb walls, FISH pointed to places of worship and served in devotional art.

A complex of meanings lead to this symbol's use. In addition, the Greek word for FISH, *IXΘYC*, is an acrostic on the first letters of the Greek words, Jesus Christ, God's Son, Savior. (John 20:31.)

Some Chrismons combine the FISH with the word *IXΘYC*. Another fish bears a basket of bread on it's back, an Eucharistic symbol that evokes other meanings as well. Three fish suggest the Triune God. Numerous fish symbolize followers of the Christ.

BUTTERFLY: Our Lord's Resurrection; Resurrection of those who die in Christ. I Corinthians 15: 20-23.

DESCENDING DOVE: The Holy Spirit at our Lord's baptism. Mark 1:10

LAMB: A Scriptural Symbol for Christ.

SERPENT ON TAU CROSS: Prefiguration of the sacrifice on the Cross. John 3:14

SAND DOLLAR (Holy Ghost Shell): Marking recall events in Jesus' life.

SCALLOP SHELL with Three Drops of Water: Baptism in the Name of the Three Persons. Matthew 28:19.

PEARL: Word of God. Matthew 7:6; 13:45.

IVORY: Our Lord's Body. Solomon 5:14.

16

ARTIFACTS

SCROLL: Prophecy; Pentateuch; Scripture. FOUR SCROLLS : The Four Gospels.

BOOK: The written Word. The Bible. As symbols, the Book and the Scroll are frequently interchangeable. SIXTY-SIX BOOKS: The Bible.

BREAD: The Christ. John 6:48 ff.

BREAD, CHALICE (Cup) : Either or both. The Last Supper; Holy Communion. Mark 14:22 ff; I Corinthians 11:23 ff.

CROWN: The Kingship of our Lord; His victory over sin and death; His place of honor at the right hand of God the Father. I Timothy 6:15; Revelation 14:14; Romans 8:34.

FIERY CHARIOT: Ascension of our Lord. II Kings 2 :11; Acts 1:9-11.

LAMP: Divine inspiration; Truth; Knowledge. Psalms 43:3; 119:105. TEN LAMPS: The ten virgins.

LIGHT: Our Lord : "I am the light of the world." John 8:12. Father: "Believe . . . that you may become sons of light." John 12:36; Psalm 27:1.

LIGHTS: Our Lord's followers, "You are the light of the world ." Matthew 5:14

MANGER: The Nativity of the Christ. Often with a nimbus to suggest the divinity of the Child. Luke 2:7 ff .

SHEPHERD'S CROOK: Our Savior, "I am the good shepherd." John 10:11 ff. OR, the shepherds at the manger.

Numbers

Numbers connote meanings only when one understands their reference. Thus, numbers are not symbols but signs that point to certain ideas. These ideas are the real elements that enter into the meaning of a specific Chrismon. Figures themselves are not on Chrismons. One finds them by counting points, lines or other like elements. The resulting number indicates the idea to consider. The design above, composed of three fish-shaped forms, symbolizes one God in three Persons.

1 Unity of the Godhead. One God.

2 The two Natures of our Lord, human and divine. Or, the known but still unseen God.

3 The Triune God; Persons of the Godhead. Heaven.

4 The earth; the four corners of the earth. The four Gospels; the four Evangelists.

5 The five wounds of our Lord. Epiphany of the Lord. The Pentateuch.

6 God the Father Creator; Days of creation. The attributes of the Messiah. Isaiah 11:2.

7 Gifts of the Spirit. Revelation 5:12. The perfect number, 3 + 4: Union of heaven and earth.

8 Holy Baptism; Regeneration. Or, "Eighth" day of creation: Resurrection of our Lord. Completion.

9 Fruits of the Spirit. Galatians 5:22.

10 The Ten Commandments. Ten virgins.

12 The Apostles; the Church; the Tribes of Israel.

FIGURES

An equilateral **TRIANGLE** is a figure made up of three separate but equal sides. Any design of three equal parts may symbolize the Holy Trinity, one God in three Persons. A figure for the Triune may be combined with another. Adding a circle, for example points out the eternal nature of the Trinity. Or, two different symbols for the Triune God may be superimposed.

CIRCLE: Eternity; God the only eternal One; God 's eternal love; or eternal life with God .

ORB (BALL): In ancient times, the heavens around the earth; more recently, earth alone.

SQUARE: An older figure for the earth or earthly things. Note that a square has four sides.

The number of SIDES or PARTS of any geometric figure implies a definite element. Page 18 lists interpretations based on numbers.

VESICA PISCIS: An almond or fish like shape that abstractly suggests our Lord and God.

NIMBUS: A circle of light around the head that connotes Godliness or holiness.

TRI-RADIANT NIMBUS: Three rays of light in a nimbus indicate a Person of the Triune.

CRUCIFORM NIMBUS: The sign of the cross in the circle denotes the crucified Christ.

GLORY: A combination of the nimbus and rays of light to suggest the atmosphere in which God lives. It generally surrounds the whole figure.

TRIANGLE

TREFOIL

3 CIRCLES

TRIQUETRA

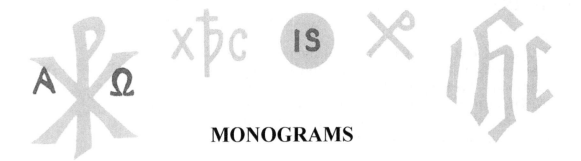

MONOGRAMS

XP or CHI RHO: Most monograms of Christ Jesus are based on Greek words, the language of the world known to the early church. In Greek, Christ (the Hebrew 'Messiah') is XPICTOC. All the monograms for Christ in the various Chrismons are derived from these letters. John 1:41.

Sometimes the first letter is alone. Or, the first and last may be used . But the most widely known Chrismon is the Chi Rho (XP), the union of the first two letters. Generally the letters are super- imposed as in the large figure at the upper left.

Changing the position and shape of the letters may evoke other meanings. The Chi may become a manger with a Rho that is a shepherd's crook. Or, the X can form a cross while the P becomes the person on it.

IHC IHS: Likewise, monograms for our Lord's given name are based on the Greek for Jesus, IHCOYC. The most used monogram is the Iota Eta Sigma (IHC or IHS). An early form of the Greek Sigma is C; the S is now used more often. The monogram may also be I, IC, or IS. Matthew 1:21-25

CIPHER: The first letters of our Lord's title, Christ, and His name, Jesus, combine to form His cipher. This design may appear alone or with another figure. Placing a circle around it symbolizes the eternal nature of the Son of Man.

A cross formed from a Chi Rho is the basis for the Chrismon at the right. The triangle (for the Holy Trinity) calls attention to the Christ's divinity while the monogram of His mother Mary (M) suggests His human birth.

iħc iħc xp̄s

The Greek sign for an abbreviation is a line over the letters. By extending an upright line from a letter, early Christians put the sign of the cross into some of our Lord's monograms.

The cross at the right shows how monograms can be hidden in a design. Among the letter combinations that are readily discernable are: XP, XPC, IC, IX, and IC XC for JESUS, THE CHRIST.

Many CORNERSTONES are on our tree. Monograms of our Savior are on their sides while the bottoms show another symbol for the "chief cornerstone ."

Ephesians 2:20; Mark 12:10.

Some Chrismons on our tree are monograms only. But generally a monogram is combined with one or more symbols for the Christ. The XP, for example, appears with the Alpha and Omega while the IHS may be on a cross.

21

LETTERS & WORDS

ALPHA & OMEGA: The first and the last letters in the Greek alphabet. Note the two forms of the Omega. "I am the Alpha and the Omega, the first and the last, the beginning and the end." Revelation 22:13; Isaiah 44:6; 48:12. This symbol of Christ's divinity is generally used with another symbol or monogram for the Lord. Sometimes, lines may be extended from the letters to form a cross.

When a middle letter of the Greek alphabet, MU, is inserted, the idea becomes, "Jesus Christ is the same yesterday and today and for ever." Hebrews 13:8.

First letters of the Latin superscription on the cross, "Jesus of Nazareth, the King of the Jews." John 19:19.

Verbum Dei Manet in AEternum .." Isaiah 40:8; I Peter 1:25.

"The Word of God Endures Forever," translation of the Latin phrase above.

The Greek word for fish, which forms an acrostic on the Greek phrase, Jesus Christ, God's Son, Savior.

The Greek word for Conqueror or Victor: Our Lord's victory over sin and death for us. I Corinthians 15:54-57.

" 'His name shall be called Emmanuel' (which means, God with us)." Matthew 1:23; Isaiah 7:14.

THE CHRISTIAN YEAR SERIES

The large double loop, or figure 8, on the front of our tree is the Christian Year Series. It explains, symbolically, our Lord's Life and the Nature of God within the framework of the Christian Year.

The upper loop proclaims the Triune God, one God who showed Himself to man in three different ways. The lower loop, read counterclockwise, shows God's most complete revelation or Himself in the Life of the Man Jesus. Pages 23 - 30 of this book explain the meaning of this connected group of Chrismons.

SEASONS SYMBOLS & CROSSES

ADVENT: Scroll with Prophecy. Coming of the Messiah Who shall bring peace. Isaiah 9:6; Luke 1:79.

TAU CROSS (Advent, Anticipatory, Old testament): Salvation Promised but not yet accomplished. Numbers 21:9; John 3:14-15.

CHRISTMAS: Gladiolus. The Incarnation, the "Word became flesh." The living sword-the living Word. John 1:1, 14; Hebrews 4:12.

ANCHOR CROSS (Cross of Hope): This Child, the hope of the world. Or, a cross rises out os the crescent moon, a symbol for Mary, our Lord's mother. Hebrews 6:19; Luke 2:7.

EPIPHANY: Five-Pointed Star. The Manfestation to the wise men. "A star out of Jacob" "I am ...the bright morning star." Matthew 2; Numbers 24:17; Revelation 22:16.

CROSS CROSSLET: Spread of Christianity to the North, East, South, and West - to the ends of the earth. Matthew 28:19; Mark 8:34; Acts 1:8.

LENT: Pelican-in-her-piety. The Atonement, Sacrifice of Christ for our sins. Lord's Supper. (Her blood feeds her young.) Psalm 102:6 (KJV); Matthew 26:26 ff.

PASSION CROSS (Cross of Suffering): Pointed ends remind us of the points of the thorns, the nails, and the spear. John 19.

EASTER: Phoenix rising from Flames. The resurrection. (From Egyptian fables: A miraculous bird destroyed itself in flames only to rise again to new life. Thus a symbol for immortality.)

> **CROSS IN GLORY** (Rayed Easter): The rising sun behind the cross suggests the new day when our Lord conquered death for us. 1 Corinthians 15:3, 4.

ASCENSION: Chariot of Fire. Our Lord's Ascension parallels Elijah's. The fiery chariot is a type for the Ascension. II Kings 2:11; Acts 1:9-11.

> **CROSS OF CONSTANTINE**: The Chi Rho with the
> X   turned to form a cross - Christ the victorious King.
> I Timothy 6:15.

PENTECOST: Seven - Tongued Flame. The Holy Spirit on the Day of Pentecost. Seven gifts of the Spirit. Acts 2:1-4; Revelation 5;12
> **CROSS FLAMANT** (Fiery cross): Flames signify the fiery zeal of one filled with the Spirit of God. Romans 12:11

FIGURES around the Symbols: A circle to suggest God and a square for the earth surrounds the season symbols that represent God's saving action in the world.

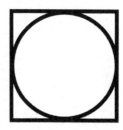

Flames of the Spirit close the Life Cycle and join it to the Trinity cycle. By the Spirit, the Life came to us, "was incarnate by the Holy Ghost." By that same Spirit, the Life comes back. But the Flames more than join the two cycles: They also reach out to us. Through the "Counselor," the Life may live in us today. Matthew 1:18 ff; Acts 1, 2; John 14; 15.

Christian Year Series

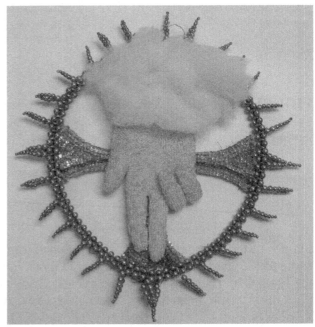

FATHER

CHALICE

SHELL

TRIUNE

SON

SPIRIT

PENTECOST

ADVENT

Prince of Peace

ASCENSION

BOOK

CHRISTMAS

EASTER

EPIPHANY

LENT

TRINITY & PERSON SYMBOLS

TRINITY: Legend says that Patrick used a SHAMROCK to help explain the mystery of One God in three Persons. Another symbol for the Holy Trinity, the TRIANGLE is entwined with a CIRCLE of GLORY to suggest the eternal nature of the Triune.

CROSS TREFLEE (Bottonnee): Three balls at the end of each arm suggest the Persons of the Triune, each of Whom act in our Salvation. II Corinthians 13:14.

The trinity complex hangs inside the upper loop, apart from the line of the figure 8 because "no one has seen God."

(John 1:18) Yet He shows Himself to man in three ways: As the Father Creator, the Savior Son, and the Spirit Sanctifier. Symbols for these Persons appear on the line of the loop. The GLORY surrounds each figure.

FATHER: Hand from Cloud. Frequently used in both the Old and New Testaments, the Hand was almost the only symbol that designated the Father during Christianity's first thousand-years. Psalm 98:1.

SON: *Agnus Dei* or Lamb of God. Derived from prophecy, the Lamb is the most enduring figure for our Lord. Reference is to the sacrificial lamb of Isreal. With the banner of Victory, it represents the risen Christ. Isaiah 53:7; Revelation 5:6.

SPIRIT: Descending Dove. Also an ancient symbol of Scriptural origin, the dove has been widely used since the days of the first Christians. Matthew 3:16.

STARS, VINE, CENSERS

STARS proclaim the ways in which God comes to us.

CHALICE on Six Pointed Star: The Lord's Supper. This Star denotes the attributes of the Messiah. Isaiah 11:2.

SHELL on Eight Pointed Star: Holy Baptism. Regeneration. I Peter 3:20; 21.

BOOK on Seven Pointed Star: The written Word. "The Word of God Endures Forever." The Star refers to the Gifts of the Holy Spirit Who inspires the Scripture.

Multi-pointed **STARS** around the Trinity symbol connote Heaven, God's element. **CENSERS** are scattered along the upper loop to suggest Prayer. Revelation 5:8.

CROSS SALTIRE: "First called" of our Lord's twelve, Andrew is said to have died on a cross of this shape. As the Church Year begins on the Sunday closest to St. Andrew's Day we use this cross to depict all who are "called," the whole Christian Church. The Church developed the way of living with our Lord which we call the Christian Year. John 1:35-42.

VINE: "No one has seen GOD; The...Son...has made Him known." A Vine connects the symbols which explain that Life, God's revelation of Himself. Nine bunches of fruit hang on the Vine, the fruit of those who abide in Christ through the Spirit of truth. May you find yourself among these fruits. John 1:18; 15; Galatians 5:22.

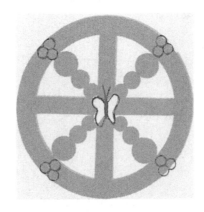

ELEMENTS COMBINED

Chrismons that contain only one or two elements are easy to "read." Even when an ornament combines several ideas, at least part of the meaning is readily apparent. But to comprehend the fullness of the story, on needs to be aware of many thoughts that may be expressed.

Not everyone receives the same message from even simple Chrismons. Nor should they! Some symbols can have a number of meanings. Furthermore, individuals, because of their varied experiences, bring differing insights. But every part of a Chrismon, even its decoration, has something specific to say about our Lord and God.

We offer interpretations to help viewers identify various elements in a Chrismon and to share the intended message. You, however, will most understand and enjoy those meanings that you discover for yourself.

Six elements combine to form the above Chrismons: Our Lord's monogram X; the sign of the Cross; a butterfly to suggest resurrection; a circle for eternity, God or eternal life; and four (earth) clusters of three balls (Holy Trinity) to denote God's action on earth.

Because of the love of the Father, the Christ became the sacrifice for our sins in His death on the cross, the Con's victory over that death may, through the Holy Spirit, become earthly man's entrance into eternal Life.

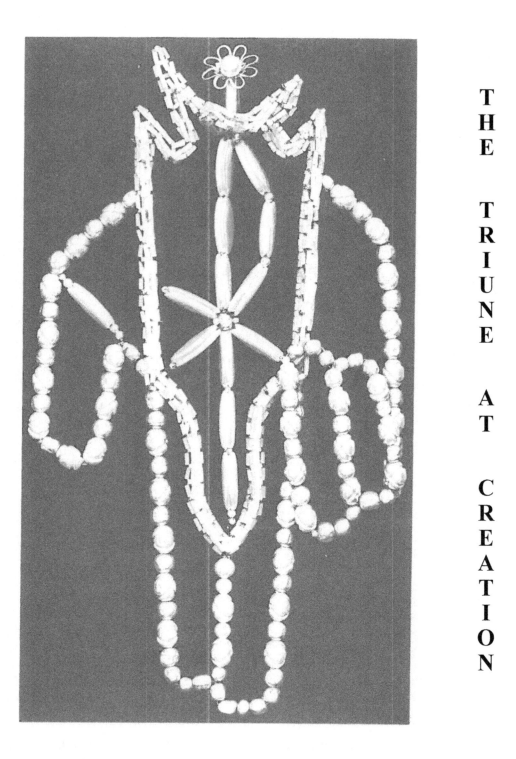

THE TRIUNE AT CREATION

A glance at this design reveals a HAND, which suggests God the Father Creator. But a closer study discloses, in the lines of the palm and fingers, the XP MONOGRAM of the Son and a DESCENDING DOVE for the Holy Spirit. The whole figure implies that, though the Father God is the Creator, all three Persons of the Triune concurred in the Act of Creation. Genesis 1:1, 26: John 1:1-18.

31

EMMANUEL: GOD WITH US

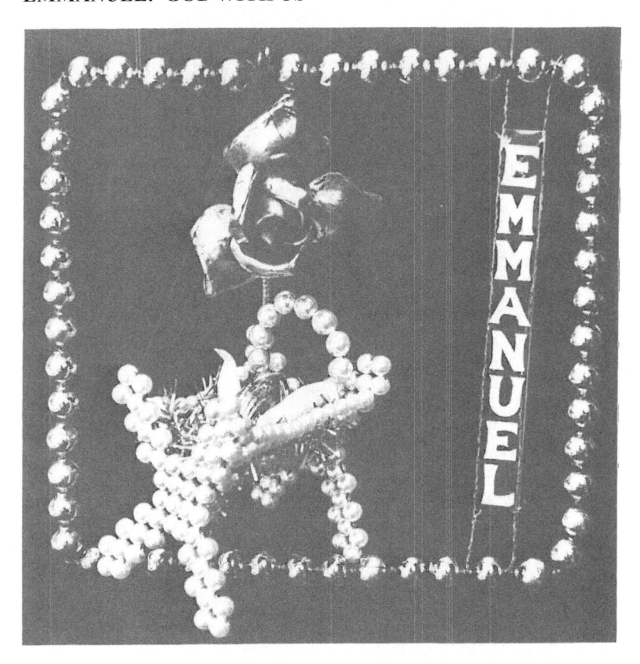

The ROSE leaning over the manger represents Mary, Jesus' mother. Inside the crib, a ROSE-BUD and a NIMBUS suggest the Child. Notice how the position of the Mother and the manger reveals the Christ's MONOGRAM, XP. A SQUARE, an ancient symbol for the earth, surrounds the scene and another name for the Child, EMMANUEL, which means, "God with us." (Matthew 1:18-25.) When the Virgin conceived and bore a Son, God was with all of us as He had never been before. Through the Person of the Child, God was with us as One of us.

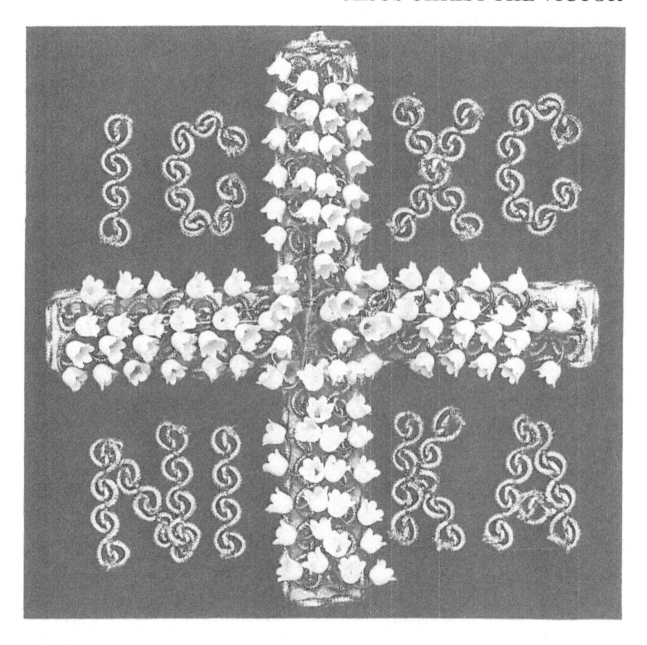

The Greek word for victor or conqueror is N I K A. A Greek monogram for our Lord's given name Jesus is IC, for His title Christ, XC. These letters surround a cross, the means of death for the Man Jesus. But, as the letters and the word state, He conquered: He rose victorious over that death and the sin that caused it. The cross became the CROSS ADORNED-a cross decorated with flowers-a symbol of the new life that He won for us.

But how did He conquer? With armies? With power? Is not that how one conquers? Not this One! LILIES-OF- THE-VALLEY adorn this cross-low-growing flowers, blossoms that bend low. This One conquered in humility.

TREES OF LIFE

The Christmas Tree itself is often considered symbolic by Christians. Because of its **EVER-GREEN** nature, it suggests eternal life. Based on the Song of Solomon (5 :15), the **CEDAR** is a figure for the Christ.

Reading meanings into this greatest of plants follows Scriptural practice. The **"TREE OF LIFE"** theme runs through the written Word from Genesis 2:9 to Revelation 22:19. Consideration of Biblical use of the tree symbol has resulted in five Chrismons called "The Trees."

**P
A
R
D
I
S
E**

**T
R
E
E**

From four roots out of God's earth this tree bears two foods: the FRUIT by which man lost paradise (Genesis 2, 3) and the fruit or BREAD by which man may regain paradise (John 6:25-59). Every man eats the first fruit. By God's mercy, every man may also eat the bread of eternal life. I Corinthians 15:20 ff.

R O S E   &   C A N D L E   T R E E

The construction of this tree reveals our Lord's dual nature and His life-giving essence. The roots are a SEVEN-POINT STAR to suggest the Holy Spirit; the flowers are ROSES to symbolize His Mother Mary: ". . . was incarnate by the Holy Ghost of the Virgin Mary." From the flowers rise the fruits, LIGHTED CANDLES: The life is the light of men . . . His light shines . . . and we behold His glory. Matthew 1:18-21; John 1:4-14.

J E S S E   T R E E

Our Lord's human ancestors. Isaiah 11:1-10; Luke 3.

Terminal
Flower: LAMB - Christ
        LILLY - Mary

Roots: SHEPHERD'S CROOK - Jesse
        SCEPTER - Tribe of Judah

RULERS OF JUDAH (Flowers on the Tree)

Lyre - David
Temple - Solomon
Ark of the Covenant - Asa
Tablets of Commandments - Jehosaphat

7 Branch Candlestick - Joash
Sundial - Hezikiah
Pentateuch - Josiah
Fig in Chains - Jehoiakim
Plummet - Zerubbabel

THE TRUE VINE

Our Lord and His divine family, the Church .
CROSS TRIUMPHANT: The world united in Christ. Roots-THREE FISH-"The Father loves you . . .
Glorify thy Son . . . Spirit of truth will guide you ." John 14, 15, 16, and 17.

THE APOSTLES (Branches bearing Fruit) Acts 1:13, 26.

Cross & Bread - Phillip	Book & Fish - Simon	Serpent in Chalice - John
Crossed Keys - Peter	Cross Saltire - Andrew	Shell & Sword - James
Money Bags - Matthew	Saw - James the Less	Ship - Jude
Book & Axe - Matthias	Scimitar - Bartholemew	Square & Spear - Thomas

Cut off Branch - Judas

T H E   C R U C I F I X

THE PARADOX TREE: The Tree of Death-the Tree of Life "He himself bore our sins in his body on the tree, that we might die to sin and live to righteousness . By his wounds you have been healed." I Peter 2:24. Also see Matthew 12:33; Deuteronomy 21:22, 23; Galatians 3:13.

OUR LORD'S MINISTRY

For some days after our Lord's resurrection from the death of the cross, He continued to serve. As He had throughout the three years of His public ministry, the Christ manifested His Person; He preached and taught; and He healed. Then, having given His apostles proof of His Being, the Son returned to His heavenly Father.

Chrismons that depict our Savior's ministry fall into two groups: Those that suggest miracles which Jesus of Nazareth worked to help people and to show His power, and Chrismons that portray His teachings.

SERPENT ON TAU CROSS: Jesus of Nazareth's chief mission was, of course, the reconciliation of man and God. His sacrifice on the cross makes that reunion possible. Early in His ministry, our Savior explained the how and why of that reconciliation with a reference to an event in Jewish history, the serpent on Moses' staff. The Christ's greatest healing miracle is that from the cross-the staff- "the tree of life . . . for the healing of nations."
Romans 5:6-11 ; John 4:14-21; Numbers 21:4 ff; Revelation 22:2, 14.

THE FIRST MIRACLE

HIS MIRACLES

When Jesus turned water into wine at the wedding in Cana, He demonstrated His concern for the whole man. At the left, six water JARS symbolize this miracle. ROSES at their base point to our Lord 's humanity. The MOUNDED CROSS has the same meaning as the Cross Triumphant. The VINE for Christ runs into branches, two of which denote the couple. Interlacing the RINGS in the CHRISTOGRAM suggests marriage in Christ. The DOVE portrays the Spirit bestowing His gifts. John 2:1-11.

H
E
A
L
I
N
G

CROSS POTENT: In Biblical times and in primitive areas today, a crutch is shaped like a letter T. Thus, this cross, composed of four "crutches," became a symbol for the Savior's physical and spiritual healing powers. In the miracle designated above, Jesus healed a man of his sins as well as of his paralysis. Matthew 9:2-8.

OUR LORD'S TEACHINGS:

The Parable Balls

Jesus taught in parables. "Indeed," Matthew reported, "He said nothing . . . without a parable." (13:34) These Chrismons depict Christ's teachings in His figurative language. Although not all of them derive from full length parables, each ball does represent a spoken symbol that our Lord used.

The three inch balls are scattered over our tree. For easier identification, the balls that portray Jesus' teachings about the Father God are gold. Christ's words about Himself, the "Son" (I am") balls are white. Parables that proclaim the Kingdom of God hang in open balls of three concentric circles.

On Kingdom balls of woven bead circles (right below), a gold circle made of six point stars suggests the Father; a white circle of five point stars denotes the Son; and curved flames centered with a seven point star symbolize the Spirit. The colors of those balls of single bead circles (shown above) are the same except for the Spirit circle, which is of clear material.

Kingdom ball above: "A wise man who built his house upon the rock." Matthew 7:24.

From the left below:

Father: "Consider the ravens . . . the lilies." Luke 12:24.

Son: "As a shepherd separates the sheep." Matthew 25:32.

Kingdom: "Pearl of great value." Matthew 13:45.

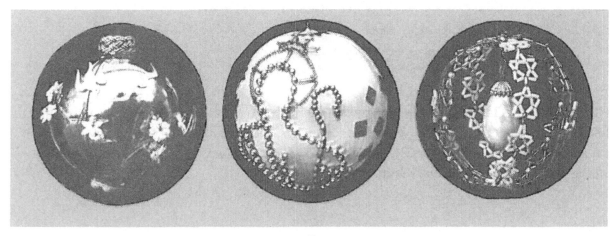

Gold Father Balls

TREE, SPADE:
The Barren fig tree. Luke 13:6 ff.

PLAIN BALL:
"Worship the father in spirit . . . God is spirit."
John 4:23 ff.

NIMBED FIGURE of the SON:
He who has seen me has seen the Father."
John 14:8 ff.

MANSION :
"In my Father's house are many rooms." John 14:2 ff.

MAN RUNNING to HOUSE in MOONLIGHT:
"A friend . . . at midnight." Luke 11:5 ff.

BUTTERFLIES, SQUARE:
"A king who gave a marriage feast for his son." Matthew 22:1 ff.

SHEARS, VINE:
"My father is the vinedresser." John 15: 1 ff.

MAN with OPEN ARMS:
The father of the prodigal son. Luke 15:11 ff.

PEARLS FENCED IN with ONE OUTSIDE:
"Ninety-nine and the one sheep." Matthew 18:12 ff.

BALANCE:
King who forgave a servant who later was unmerciful.
Matthew 18:23 ff.

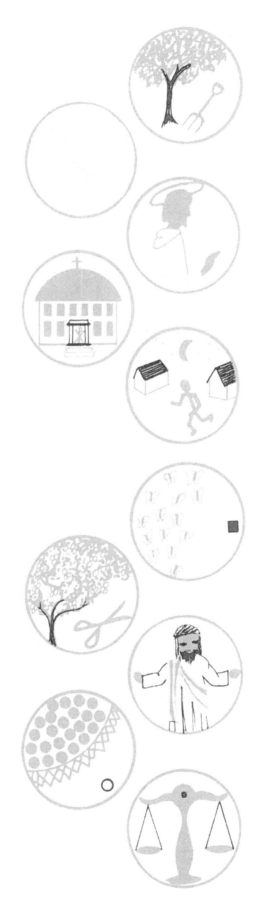

White Son Balls

DOOR :
"I am the door; if any one enters . . ." John 10:9.

CHRISTOGRAM RADIATING LIGHT:
"I am the light of the world." John 8:12; 11:9 ff.

STONE WITH XP:
"The stone which . . . has become the head of the corner." Luke 20 :17.

WHEAT FROM CROSS, LOAF OF BREAD:
"I am the bread of life." John 6:48 ff.

PATH, LAMP, BUTTERFLY:
"I am the way, the truth, and the life."
John 1 4:6 .

VINE WITH CHRISTOGRAM ROOTS:
"I am the true vine." John 15:1 ff.

BASIN, TOWEL: "I am your servant . . . your slave."
John 13:4 ff; Matthew 20:26 ff .

CADUCEUS IN FISH:
"The well have no need of a physician, but I came . . ."
Mark 2 :17.

COINS:
"I am like the master who gave talents."
Matthew 25:14 ff.

S T R E A M S OF WATER FROM ROCK:
"I give living water." (KJV) John 4:10 ff; 7:37 ff.

44

Open Kingdom Balls

VARIED BEADS :
"A great banquet." Luke 14:15 ff .

CHILDREN:
"Let the children come . . . receive . . . like a child ."
Mark 10:13 ff .

ROCKS, BIRDS, THORNS, FULL GROWN WHEAT:
"Sower sowing seed." Mark 4:3 ff .

WHEAT GROWING:
"First the blade then the ear . . . "Mark 4 :26 ff.

TREE, SEED:
"Like a grain of mustard seed." Mark 4:30 f.

BEADS THROUGHOUT THE BALL:
"Like leaven . . . hid in . . . meal " Luke 13:21.

FISHES IN NET:
"Like a net . . . in to the sea. " Matthew 13:47.

GOLD, BLACK BLADES
"Wheat and weeds." Matthew 13: 24 ff.

TEN LAMPS:
"Ten virgins." Matthew 25:1 ff.

LARGE CROSS, SMALL CROSSES:
"Let him . . . take up his cross daily." Luke 14:47 ff.

MIRROR:
"The kingdom of God is within you." (KJV) Luke 17:20 f.

Beatitudes

These Chrismons depict the happy ones of the Kingdom of God whom our Lord calls blessed . Each "Beatitude" has two parts: A triad to symbolize the Triune God and His Kingdom forms the outer part; another design, which identifies a specific blessed one, hangs inside.

The **TRIAD** doesn't cut the happy ones off from the world. Instead its open design allows outsiders to touch the central symbol just as the symbol can easily move to the outer area. The triad is like an aura that sets the blessed ones apart in spirit only. For, though the happy ones who have responded to God 's call are not of this world, they are very much in it. John 17:11-26.

The triads, same for all the Beatitudes, are composed of:

An EYE in gold: The glory and majesty of the omniscient Father and His ever-watchful , loving care.

A FISH in white: The purity of the Son, our Savior.

A DESCENDING DOVE of transparent material: The Holy Spirit Whose gift we receive in Holy Baptism.

Yet, because the blessed are new persons in Christ, their actions and reactions in the world are new too. The inner symbol of each "Beatitude" describes activities and / or responses of these happy ones. II Corinthians 5:16 ff.

"Blessed are the poor in spirit (Phillips translation: humble minded), for theirs is the kingdom of heaven.

LILIES-OF-THE-VALLEY

"Blessed are those who mourn, for they shall be comforted.

TEARS IN A TEAR

"Blessed are the meek, for they shall inherit the earth.

GLOBE OF THE WORLD

"Blessed are those who hunger and thirst for righteousness, for they shall be satisfied

WHEAT AND GRAPES

Blessed are the merciful, for they shall obtain mercy.

BALANCE

"Blessed are the pure in heart, for they shall see God.

HEART

"Blessed are the peacemakers, for they shall be called sons of God .

OLIVE BRANCH

"Blessed are those who are persecuted for righteousness' sake, for theirs is the kingdom of heaven." Matthew 5:3-10.

MARTYDOM SYMBOLS

47

ANGELS & ARCHANGELS

Winged beings suggest the spirits that God created to praise and serve Him. As God-sent messengers, **ANGELS** told men of the Birth, Resurrection, and Ascension of His Son. (Matthew 1:20, 21; Luke 2:9 ff; John 20:12; Acts 1:10, 11.) The Gospels also tell how angels ministered to their Lord and ours during His Life on earth. (Mark 1:13; Luke 22:43.)

Portraying these beings as winged symbolizes the fact that, as spirits, angels can go anywhere. Showing them in human form implies that they can communicate with man. Specifically, herald angels symbolize the Nativity of our Lord and God's redeeming Love.

In the position of each angel on our tree, one can see a sign for our Savior. Some form a Chi (X), an Iota (I), or a cross. Or, two angels may join to spell out the Chi Rho (illustrated on this page), XC, IC, or IX.

The **ARCHANGELS** pictured on page 49 hang around the Creche on our tree. As the Annunciation angel, GABRIEL wears a cope and holds a lily. MICHAEL, militant protector, is in armor. (Luke 1:19, 26 ff; Daniel 12:1; Revelation 12:7.)

The Apocrypha names the other archangels. A staff and gourd identify RAPHAEL, by tradition the angel who proclaimed our Lord's birth to the shepherds. Indicated by a scroll, URIEL, which means "God is my light," is said to have watched over Jesus' tomb. (Matthew 28:2 ff.)

GABRIEL

URIEL

RAPHAEL

MICHAEL

CHRISMONS FOR EVERYONE

From a one-time, volunteer Christmas tree in a small Church in 1957, the Chrismon tree has become a worldwide celebration and proclamation of our Lord's Name and His saving acts. Individuals and groups of all denominations have been using Chrismons in their worship, educational, and social activities throughout the year. We're grateful that we have been able to contribute our Chrismon know -how to this witness. And we thank God for the many Chrismon users and makers who have kept us busy in this work .

The Chrismon program requires personal doing. One cannot buy the ornaments but makes them according to his or her own abilities and needs. As we have from the beginning of the program, we share our patterns and instructions for making these Christian ornaments.

The directions are so complete that men, women, and teenagers have followed them successfully. Even children, with some parental supervision, can make their own Chrismons. No particular skill is needed-just the willingness to use one's hands to praise the Christ.

At present, the available directions consist of four separate books or Series: *The Basic Series* presents patterns for monograms and symbols for our Lord and God. The thirty designs in this group are more than enough to decorate any tree. Because certain information in this Series isn't repeated in the other books, one should have the Basic to understand everything in the other Series.

Chrismons for E very Day may be a companion to the Basic book for beginners or a source of more than thirty new Chrismon tree designs and specific workshop guides for more advanced workers. But the book's main focus is in showing ways to use Chrismons throughout the year. Instructions for wedding cake toppers, arrangements, pictures, mobiles, bookmarks, and wreaths are included.

The Christian Year Series combines varied symbols based on seasons of the Church Year. As a unit, the Series provides a focal point for the tree or seasonal education around the year. When made up as individual Chrismons, the thirty designs are used in the same manner as the Basic ornaments.

Several sets of Chrismons as well as individual symbols make up the more than sixty decorations in the *Advanced* book. No designs are duplicated in any of the Series.

Each book of instructions contains directions and patterns for making the Chrismons in that Series. When size reduction is advisable for home use, we give home-size as well as the original church-size patterns. Also included are interpretations for every symbol; a worship program to explain the meaning of Chrismons in that Series; photographs, most at least one-third actual size, of the ornaments in that group; sources of materials for making Chrismons; and additional information on how to use and make the Series.

During the 25th anniversary year of the Chrismon tree at Ascension, a 170 page history of the program, *Chrismons: The First 25 Years,* was published. The book, by Frances Kipps Spencer, originator of the Chrismons, describes the conception and development of the Chrismon program at Ascension, across the nation, and around the world. In addition, it includes illustrations and photographs of Chrismon trees, and people active in various aspects of the Chrismon project world-wide.

Purchase of the instructions does not entitle anyone to make Chrismons for sale. We never give this permission. A copyright release, necessary to make the widest use of the Chrismon idea, is given to churches and non-profit institutions on request and at no charge.

Secular groups, congregations, families, and individuals use the Chrismons-use them not only at Christmas time but throughout the year-as an aid to know and proclaim the Christ. We enjoy the Christian fellowship that this participation has brought to us all. If we may be of any further help to you in using the Chrismon program in your situation, please feel free to call on us at any time. Just address your inquiries to the Chrismon Committee in care of our Church.

INDEX OF SYMBOLS AND SEASONS

"Now to him who is able...to the only God. Our Savior through Jesus Christ our Lord, be glory, majesty, dominion, and authority, before all time and now and for ever."

Jude 24, 25.

Made in the USA
Las Vegas, NV
05 October 2021

31780709R00033